Introduction to Pendulum Dowsing
Learn How to Dowse with a Pendulum

Carole Anne Somerville

Copyright 2017 Carole A Somerville

All rights reserved. No part of this publication may be reproduced, stored in or introduced into a retrieval system, or transmitted, in any form, or by any means (electronic, mechanical, photocopying, recording, or otherwise) without the prior written permission of the copyright owner.

ISBN-13: 9781520647449

Spiritual Development Workbooks

Nurture your Mind, Body, Soul & Spirit
Tap into your Psychic Self
Build your Spiritual Muscles

This Workbook will introduce you to everything you need to know to be able to read a Pendulum with confidence.

I would recommend that you start a Journal before you begin reading this book in which you can record results of exercises, dreams and intuitive experiences.

I hope you will enjoy this fun and insightful journey.

"Lots of things are mysteries. But that doesn't mean there isn't an answer to them. It's just that scientists haven't found the answer yet." ~ Mark Haddon, 'The Curious Incident of the Dog in the Night-Time

Contents:

Lesson 1: What is a Pendulum – How to Choose, Cleanse and Charge your Pendulum
Lesson 2: How to Program your Pendulum – Preparing yourself and your pendulum to give a reading
Lesson 3: How to Use your Pendulum – Asking questions of your pendulum
Lesson 4: The Many Uses of a Pendulum – How pendulums can be used to find missing items, answer questions and to detect weaknesses in the body
Lesson 5: How do you Approach Pendulum Dowsing? – Tips for using your pendulum
Lesson 6: Giving Pendulum Readings – What to consider when giving pendulum readings
Lesson 7: Pendulum Charts – How to design and use pendulum Charts
Lesson 8: How to use your Pendulum for Spiritual Development
Lesson 9: Frequently Asked Questions about Pendulum Dowsing

One
What is a Pendulum?
How to Choose, cleanse and Charge your Pendulum

A pendulum is a tool to help you connect with the collective unconscious and your Higher Self. Anyone can dowse and it can be great fun to receive yes/no answers and test your intuitive skills. It does however take a little practice. You can't expect to pick up your pendulum and receive instant correct answers. There's a bit more to it than that and in this Workbook I'll be talking you through all you need to do, to prepare yourself and your pendulum for finding answers and giving Pendulum Readings. As you follow these instructions and join in the exercises you will also be forming a bond with your pendulum.

What is a Pendulum?

A Dowsing Pendulum is an object suspended on a cord which is used to obtain information our minds cannot access on a conscious level. Pendulums can be made out of a variety of materials such as crystals, wood, metal or simple objects you can find in your home like a ring, a key or a needle. Purpose made Pendulums have shapes and geometry that are complimentary to Pendulum readings.

Pendulum dowsing is a form of divination. A question is asked of the pendulum and the answer is determined by its swing.

Pendulums have been used for dowsing and divination for centuries. Ancient kings and queens such as Cleopatra, Solomon and Sheba employed the services of psychics who practiced Radiesthesia (a sensitivity which enabled a person to detect things with the aid of a divining rod or pendulum). The Roman historian Ammianus Marcellinus described how ancient Romans used pendulums for divination and the French seer Nostradamus is said to have used a pendulum for divining.

In modern times, many psychics use pendulums for additional insight when looking for answers during their readings or to find objects. Some people just enjoy experimenting with pendulums and you can approach this method of dowsing in whichever way appeals to you. You might be curious, you might want to see if you can use pendulums to connect with your Higher Self or you might want to include the use of a pendulum in your day-to-day activities.

On saying this, remember that everyone has their own freewill and you should be discriminating in your use of your pendulum. Enjoy asking questions and building a bond with your pendulum but respect that the Universe will not take away your freewill and will encourage you, when it is necessary, to 'make your own mind up.' Just as it isn't good to seek tarot or use other forms of divination repeatedly to find answers to the same question, respect these wonderful tools and don't abuse them.

Pendulum dowsing does not have to cost a lot. You can make your own pendulum and you can buy pendulums quite cheaply. We have been asked in our workshops: what is the best pendulum for me? And: my pendulum is just a cheap one, will it work? This book will discuss how to choose your pendulum. The Universe does not distinguish between a pendulum that costs pennies and a one that is worth a fortune. If it responds to your energy vibration, it will work for you. Your pendulum can be as pricy or as inexpensive as you want it to be.

Using the pendulum can help you tune into your intuition and develop your psychic skills.

Pendulum Dowsing or Pendulum Divining?

Are you using your pendulum for dowsing or for divining? Is there a difference?

Pendulum Dowsing refers to using your pendulum to locate water, find an object, missing person or animal, missing keys or lost items of jewellery. Dowsing is using tools or our intuition to obtain information beyond the scope of our usual senses. Rhadomancy is the proper term for dowsing for hidden items … for 'finding things'. Radiesthesia also refers to finding lost items and can refer, too, to medical dowsing.

Divining is another word that some people use instead of or alongside 'pendulum dowsing.' Divining means to perceive information through intuition or insight or to use or practice divination or prophesy.

How does Pendulum Dowsing Work?

As you hold the chain with your finger tips and concentrate on your question, the pendulum becomes a direct link to your unconscious. The unconscious is where your memories are stored (from this life and past lives), it is your link to your intuition and psychic self: your Higher Self. Your Higher Self is able to connect with Divine/Universal energy. The pendulum can connect you with your Psychic side.

We have been asked: Is the pendulum moved by spirit? The answer is: 'no.' The pendulum is moved through its connection with that part of the mind where your dreams, emotions and spiritual perceptions are stored. – We can all develop a heightened awareness of our subconscious minds and using a pendulum can help us read messages from our Higher Selves that our conscious mind does not know. This in turn helps the conscious and subconscious work in harmony.

What can a Pendulum be used for?

People use pendulums for many reasons including: help with making decisions, finding lost objects or people, locating earth energies, health purposes and finding natural underground sources such as water or oil. Pendulum dowsing can also be used to uncover hidden answers, consider romantic compatibility and determine foods that may cause allergic responses. A pendulum can be a useful tool in Chakra healing, Reiki and for cleansing negative energy in a room. Some people will use a pendulum to ask the sex of an unborn baby. Ethical and legal issues should always be determined if and when using your pendulum for others and of course, yourself.

Choosing a Pendulum

You may already have a pendulum. You can make your own pendulum quite easily too. If you are thinking of buying a pendulum, there are many kinds to choose from. Think of the material first: are you drawn to crystal, brass, wood? What shape will you prefer? Pyramid, spherical, star shaped, tear-dropped, spiral or orbs?

Pendulums come in different materials, shapes, weight and sizes and every pendulum will feel different and have its own motion and energy. For instance, orbs, ovals and pointed-egg-shaped pendulums tend to swing very easily with a natural grace. Thin, pointed pendulums can take a little longer to get a momentum.

No pendulum type works better than another and it all comes down to choosing a pendulum that resonates with your energy and feels right for you.

You might have a basic idea of the type of pendulum you want: maybe a rose quartz crystal or a brass pendulum or even a wooden one. You may want something simple or ornate, tear-drop, conical or spiral. You might prefer an amethyst ball sphere pendulum or a chakra dowsing pendulum. Or you might just want to take a look at what's on the market and make your choice from all the options available.

Many people who attend our workshops have a number of pendulums; some have quite a collection, and they will choose a one they feel drawn to at the time, from which to work with. Whether you prefer to use one pendulum all the time or have a few to choose from, again, it is up to individual preference.

The best advice when choosing a pendulum is to choose the pendulum that you feel intuitively drawn too. Choose the one that calls to you. You can find some great pendulums on the internet if you don't have any New Age stores nearby that sell them. Spend some time looking at the photograph and sensing whether you feel intuitively drawn to the pendulum. If you can visit a store in person and see all the different pendulums hanging on a display rack or behind glass, this is even better. Take your time making your choice. Which one catches your eye? Pick it up and hold it in the palm of your hand. What do you feel? Does your hand feel warm while you hold it, is there a slight tingling? Close your eyes and try to imagine yourself using the pendulum. Does it feel right for you?

Wait a few moments and if you feel nothing, then move on to another one and keep trying this until you feel you have found the pendulum that's right for you. If you are able to test this pendulum to see if it responds to you, try to block out your surroundings. Now pick up the chain/string end and hold it lightly between your index finger and thumb. Keep still. Now does anything happen? Does it look as if the pendulum is moving slightly? Can you feel a slight vibration? Does it start swinging? If so, you are likely to have a good bond with your pendulum. But if it doesn't move and you still feel this is the pendulum you want to work with that's okay too. This is your choice and as you start working together your energies will align.

Once you've bought your pendulum, carry it around with you so it picks up on your energy.

How to Make a Pendulum

If you do not yet own a pendulum or haven't a one with you on your travels but would like to consult a pendulum, it can be very simple to make one.

You will need a chain on which to suspend the weight. This can be a chain from a shop that sells necklaces, or a length of string, thread wool or cord. I have also made pendulums using ribbons.

You will need a bob which is the weight at the lower end of the chain. This can be a key or a ring for instance.

Cut the cord to your desired length. You might prefer a shorter cord or you might cut it at around 18 to 24 inches (which when doubled over will be about 9 inches or a 12 inch ruler's length when in use)

You might use a necklace chain for this.

Open the clasp of the chain. Insert the open chain or one end of the cord into the hole of the object you are using (the top of a key or the inside of a ring)

Fasten the clasp or tie the cord.

Do likewise with a piece of string or wool, fastening the ends securely once they have been attached to the weight.

Caring for your Pendulum

You will be programing your pendulum - which as you work with it, will attune to your energy – so it isn't recommended that you share your pendulum with others.

You might want to store your pendulum with your cards, crystals and other tools if you are a psychic reader. Store it in a special box or wrap it in its own cloth or pouch when it is not in use. Keep it somewhere where other people won't be touching it or the pendulum might pick up their energy and this will confuse your answers.

Clearing your Pendulum

Before you start using your pendulum which you may have bought, made or received as a gift, you need to clear your pendulum of all the energies it has absorbed from other people who have handled it already. This is very easy to do.

Why does a Pendulum need cleansing? Most pendulums are made from natural materials such as crystals or wood that come from Mother Earth. They hold nature's energy and magnetic/electrical energy fields within. These materials are then taken from their natural settings for a variety of purposes. Once removed from their natural setting, gems, crystals, wood, stone … these materials made from the earth's elements that are used for psychic work … need to be cleansed and energized regularly.

So, as with other divining tools, your pendulum will need to be cleansed and charged regularly. Cleanse your pendulum before and after each use.

There are a number of ways you can cleanse your pendulum (and other spiritual tools) so experiment until you find the one that you prefer.

Method 1

Choose a day when the Sun is shining.

Place the pendulum outside in the sunlight for the whole day.

As the Sun begins to set, retrieve your pendulum and bring it back indoors.

Hold the pendulum in the palm of your hand and you should be able to sense if the pendulum is cleansed.

If the pendulum feels heavy or fuzzy, you might want to repeat this process on the following day until your pendulum feels light and clear.

Method 2

You will need your pendulum, incense (Sage or Sandalwood or alternatively Lavender or Frankincense or even an incense of your choice) and an incense holder.

Choose a quiet place where you won't be disturbed.
Relax and clear your mind.
Focus your intent. You might ask your Guides, the Angels or whichever Divinity you believe in to guide you in the cleansing of your pendulum.
Light the incense.
Ask that your pendulum be cleansed.
Hold the pendulum in the palm of your hand for a few moments.
Now pass the pendulum slowly through the incense smoke while saying a few words of cleansing such as "Please bless this pendulum in my hand. It should bring no harm to anyone. With positive energy it shall fill, bringing only answers that are real."
Pass the pendulum through the incense smoke three times.

Every time the pendulum passes through the smoke, restate your intent.

If the pendulum feels light and clear, the cleansing is complete. If it feels heavy, repeat the cleansing.

Allow the incense to burn itself out.

Thank your guides/angels

Quick ways to cleanse your pendulum. Either:

- Burn sage and pass your pendulum through the smoke several times
- Or burn incense of your choice and pass the pendulum through the smoke
- Stand your pendulum on a windowsill or outside where it can absorb the energy of the Full Moon
- Bury your pendulum in the earth for a day and a night
- Pass the pendulum through running water (a natural stream or tap water)
- Hang it so it can absorb the Sun's rays and energy for a full day
- Soak it in water that has natural sea salt in it
- Place your pendulum in a container of sea salt for an hour

Note of caution: If your pendulum is a coated metal or the chain of your pendulum is a coated metal it may begin to corrode if you use salt solution.

Once you have cleansed your pendulum, hold it in the palm of your hand and sit quietly for a few moments to help the pendulum align with your energies.

As with other divining tools, your pendulum needs to be cleansed and charged regularly.

Charging your Pendulum

Method 1

Sit for a few minutes with your pendulum. Focus on your breathing and relax.

Calm your mind.

Focus on your intent (which is to charge your pendulum).

Hold your cleansed pendulum in the palm of your dominant hand.

Focus your thoughts on your pendulum and direct positive energy towards your divining tool holding on to the intention of charging your pendulum

Imagine energy as a white light beaming down into the pendulum.

If the pendulum begins to vibrate with your energies, the charge is complete.

Or when you feel ready, know that your pendulum has been charged.

Method 2

Light a candle. Once your pendulum is cleansed and you feel ready, hold your pendulum above the candle. Direct your gaze at your pendulum and imagine positive, healing energy flowing from the candle directly into your pendulum. See this energy as a white light beaming down and surrounding and filling your pendulum. You might feel the pendulum start to vibrate with this energy charge.

If you wish, you can ask your guides or angels to help and support you whenever you use your pendulum and that you receive answers for your highest good and the highest good of anyone you are reading for.

Method 3

You can use another crystal to energise your pendulum.

Place your pendulum on another, larger crystal such as a large quartz crystal cluster.

This method will clear any negative energy around your pendulum and will recharge your pendulum.

When using this method remember to cleanse and recharge the larger quartz crystal regularly.

Method 4

Light a candle.

Pass your pendulum over the flame three times.

Now call on the four elements to charge your pendulum.

You might use the words: "Earth element I call on you to charge this pendulum. Fire element I call on you to charge this pendulum. Air element I call on you to charge this pendulum. May this pendulum be charged by the Water element."

Leave the candle to burn in a safe place near to your pendulum so its light falls onto the pendulum while it is burning.

Sunlight

Just as the energy of the Sun cleanses pendulums and crystals, sunlight can also recharge your pendulum. Leaving your pendulum to soak in the sunlight for four or five hours can reenergise your divining tool.

Activating your Pendulum

Especially if yours is a crystal pendulum you will need to activate the crystal. Sometimes a crystal can be a 'sleeper', its energy neutral and it needs to be informed that your crystal will be used for divining purposes.

As you make a spiritual connection with your pendulum, this will help to activate (awaken) the crystal. Hold your pendulum in the palm of your hands, carry it wherever you go, handle it regularly so it aligns itself with your energy and intention to use it as a divining tool.

You can also activate your pendulum by lighting a candle, holding the pendulum over the candle flame and stating your intent to use it as a diving tool. This simple ritual will mark the initiation of your pendulum.

When not in use

Keep your Pendulum safe when it is not in use. You might choose to wear it on a neck chain and this will help it pick up your energy and strengthen the bond between you and your Pendulum. Or you might have a special box or pouch to store it in.

Psychic Workout

Get to know your Pendulum and think of it as a friend.
Consistent use of the Pendulum is said to forge a connection with your personal energy.

Two
How to Program your Pendulum
Preparing yourself and your pendulum to give readings

Preparing Yourself to Read a Pendulum

When you work with your pendulum, you need to be in the moment. It's no good having your mind on what you're going to cook for dinner or whether your favourite football team will win the match on Saturday. You need to be focused entirely on what you are doing. It can help to meditate and calm your mind before you start to use your pendulum. Choose a time and place where you know you will not be distracted.

The Importance of Grounding

The first step to any spiritual practice is grounding. Grounding keeps your energy balanced and it can be useful too throughout the day, no matter what you are doing, to ground regularly.

When we work with our intuition and/or psychic-side, we should always strive to remain grounded.

Grounding means re-establishing your connection to the earth. You can establish grounding by using visualization exercises in sending any excess energy back to the ground. Lack of grounding makes you feel as if you are getting out of touch with reality. You might feel tipsy, dizzy and unsteady on your feet or just not connected and anxious.

There are several methods for grounding and you should choose the ones that work best for you. A straight-forward technique many people use is to visualise sending roots from your feet or your root chakra (at the base of your spine) deep into the earth, allowing you to draw energy up through your roots from the earth.

Signs of being ungrounded:

Physical: You are more clumsy than usual, bumping into furniture, dropping things, feeling uncoordinated. Accident-prone. Hands and feet feel constantly cold.
Emotional: Your mood is up and down. You feel unusually sensitive, anxious or fearful. Tearful.
Mental: You get easily confused. Can't focus. Daydream a lot. Find it hard to organise
your thoughts. You feel spaced-out or mentally dizzy.
Spiritual: Your psychic sensitivity is so high you find it hard to switch off.

Visualisation Exercise to Help you Ground

So, not just in psychic work but it can be helpful to be grounded as we go about our everyday business. The following exercise is one of my favourites and can be done whenever you feel the need to ground and always when you are doing any kind of psychic work. Eventually you will be able to do this at any time but if you are new to this, find a quiet place you won't be disturbed.
Switch off your mobile.
Close your eyes and focus on your breathing. Breathe in and out for the count of four.
Bring your attention to the base of your spine. Imagine seeing roots growing from the base of your spine (your root chakra) growing down, deep into the earth and branching out as they travel down towards the earth's core.

Visualise your roots wrapping themselves around a huge crystal.

Feel your roots being anchored securely as they wrap around the crustal.

Now draw up the earth's energy through the roots. See this energy as red light

entering your root chakra, the base of your spine.

Feel this red light fill your body. Visualise your body as being solid and strong like the trunk of a tree.

Return your attention to your breathing. You feel anchored to the earth, calm and centred.

Open your eyes. You are now grounded.

The Importance of Protection

I cannot over emphasise the importance of grounding, cleansing and protection when doing any kind of psychic work and indeed, it's a good thing to get into the habit of doing all of these regularly all through your life.

There are many reasons why we should protect our aura and our energy. We might use protection techniques to protect from psychic attack and from emotional turmoil or distress. We also need to protect ourselves from negative energies that might come our way through the people we come into contact with each day, from the environment, and from 'invisible sources' such as negative thoughts being directed our way from other people. We can also protect from physical danger.

There are many spiritual techniques to shield and protect. The quickest, most basic and easiest (and with practice this can be done in an instant) is to visualise a protective bubble of light around yourself. You can choose your favourite colour or a bubble of pure white. I have used the colour blue all my life.

You can take your time over this Protection Exercise: Take three deep breaths. Try to make each breath out longer than the breath in before it. Now imagine a Brilliant White healing light coming down from above and entering your body through your crown chakra (just above your head).

Visualise this white light filling every fibre of your being, body, mind and soul. You can use the power of your mind to make this real. If you struggle to visualise this, know that the thought is enough. Imagine that any dark spaces and corners within are being filled with white, pure, cleansing light. Try to see it. Feel it. Sense it. This might be difficult at first but after a few times you will find it easier until you find yourself able to do this in seconds.

Sense your body and mind filled with white pure light, then see it expanding out of your body and into your aura. See it surrounding your body like you are surrounded by a protective eggshell of cleansing, protective White Light. This White Light is Divine Energy. It will cleanse and protect you.

The more you do this, the less time it will take for you to feel protected. As you visualise the light within you and surrounding you, know that you are fully protected.

Protection Prayer: Light a blue candle. Close your eyes and imagine Archangel Michael coming to you. Ask AA Michael to place a Blue Bubble of protective light around you. Ask that He protects you from negative energies. Visualise AA Michael walking around you with his blue sword, gently cutting any cords and ties to anyone or anything that is not for your highest good and that have been holding you back. Then ask for Him to send a shower of white healing light over you and to protect you always.

Cloak of Protection: As you begin your day, ask Archangel Michael to draw close to you. Visualise Him in your mind's eye while doing this but don't worry if you can't visualise him. Know that He listens and is close. Now ask AA Michael to cover you with His thick Blue Cloak. See the cloak surround you from the top of your head right down to your feet. His Cloak covers every inch of your body then ask Him to protect your path with his sword and his shield. Know that you are protected.

Now let's move on to preparing your Pendulum so you are able to read with it.

Programming your Pendulum

First you will need to understand the meaning of the swings of your pendulum as this is how your pendulum will be communicating with you. The pendulum swings in front-to-back direction, side to side direction and circular movements.

To understand how to interpret these movements, you need to ask your pendulum a yes/no question for which you know the answer.

Hold your pendulum in front of you between the thumb and first two fingers of your dominant hand. The chain shouldn't be too long. Wait until the weight is still. Keep your hand and arm relaxed. Any tension can prevent energy from flowing freely so try to be as relaxed as possible. Ask the pendulum a question that should receive a yes answer, for instance: Is today a …. (whatever the day is)?, Is my name … (fill in the blank), Am I male/am I female? Notice how the pendulum responds and make a note of this. The swing may only by minor at first but this is okay as it can take a while for energy to build so the pendulum interacts with you.

Take your time over this. Now wait for the chain to stop swinging or request that your pendulum stops swinging by simply stating 'Pendulum Stop!' Once it is still, ask a few questions which should receive a no answer. Make a note of how the pendulum responds.

You can check you have a connection with your pendulum by asking "show me my 'yes' response" and it should be as above and "show me my 'no' response" and again it should be as above.

You can also ask your pendulum to show you a 'maybe' response.

Possible swings to interpret:

Front to back
Side to side
Clockwise in a circle
Counter clockwise circle

Your yes/no responses may be the same as or different from other people's and this doesn't matter as the purpose of this exercise is to determine your own swing patterns. Sometimes the swings can change after some time and if you find your pendulum is inconsistent, you may need to cleanse it and recharge it with your energy.

The more you use your pendulum the more confident you will be with your interpretations. You might also class a weak swing to be a quiet response with less percentage likelihood than a big 'enthusiastic' swing which is a loud response … higher percentage likelihood.

What Kind of Questions to Ask your Pendulum

Before asking your pendulum questions, set your intention for instance: "It is my intention to use my pendulum to receive honest answers that are for my own highest good and the highest good for others." You might also ask your angels/guides to help you build a connection with your pendulum.

Be sure the pendulum's motion is completely still between questions. Your pendulum will respond best to questions requiring yes/no answers. You can ask questions you know the answers to, as suggested above, as this can help you trust what you get and your confidence will grow. In building a relationship with your pendulum you might ask friends and loved ones to give you questions they know the answer to, again, to help you experiment and learn how to interpret the language of your pendulum. As you are working with your pendulum you are also working with your intuitive side, tapping into your intuition and developing your psychic potential.

Think carefully about how you word your questions. A question should have a definite positive, negative or neutral response for instance: "According to current energies, will I pass my examination today?"

What a Pendulum can and can't Answer

You can ask your pendulum about choices, for instance: "Is it a good idea for me to attend Jane's party?", "Is this a good gift for my girlfriend?"

You can ask your pendulum about relationships, for instance: "Will I get on well with a new colleague?" or "Can I trust Henry?"

You can ask your pendulum about your health, for instance: "Should I cut down on sugar?" or "Is stress causing my headaches?"

Some people say a pendulum cannot predict future events. There are too many variables; too many things could happen to give a precise answer. This is something you might experiment with in order to make your own decision about this. Also, you have to remember that when asking about the future, the pendulum could pick up on your own hopes and respond accordingly. If you are asking about the future and are comfortable with this, you might phrase your question in a way that shows you understand a future event is a possibility but not certainty. For instance, "Taking current energies into consideration, will I get the job I was interviewed for this morning?"

Although you might not get an accurate answer to questions about the future such as: "Will I marry Henry?" (for, many things could happen that might affect the response given), you could however get a helpful answer if you ask: "All things considered, is my relationship with Henry for my highest good at this particular time?"

You can ask your pendulum about the weather, for instance: "Will it be dry today?" … you might experiment with this and see if your answers correspond to the weather forecasters and whose is the most accurate!

Example questions to ask your Pendulum will be given later.

Tips for Using your Pendulum

Keep your pendulum close to you so it is able to absorb your energy.

Test your pendulum before using it, to check for the yes/no response to answers

Use the hand that feels most comfortable to you

Some people hold the pendulum about an inch above the palm of their opposite hand when asking it questions to get better results

Try opening and closing your hands a few times if your pendulum doesn't seem to be working very well to activate your hand chakras.

Cleanse your pendulum if you feel it is heavy or it isn't responding to your energy correctly

Remember we all have free will and should make our own choices and a pendulum should not be relied on to make decisions for you.

Exercise to learn the difference between consciously and unconsciously moving a pendulum

There will be times when you may not know if the answers you are receiving from your pendulum are from Divine/Universal energy or from your own inner hopes, wishes or expectations.

It is important to learn how to let go and still your mind while working with your pendulum. The following exercise will help you learn the difference between a response generated by universal energy and a one influenced by your expectations:

Ground and protect.

Now hold your pendulum still in front of you.

Focus on your pendulum and ask it to swing in a clockwise direction, keeping your hand very still.
Stare at your pendulum and say 'clockwise' repeatedly until the pendulum starts to move in a clockwise direction.

Hold your pendulum still.

Now focus on your pendulum and ask it to swing an in anti-clockwise direction as above.
Notice how you can control the swing of the pendulum by tuning into its energy. It can be quite amazing to watch this and it helps you realise how your mind has to be clear when asking for answers so you are not influencing your pendulum.

How to clear your mind before giving a pendulum reading

Relax. Now repeat a simple mantra in your head over and over. This will help your thoughts from wandering. Keep repeating the mantra and by clearing your mind of all wayward thoughts you are allowing yourself and your pendulum to be receptive to the Universal energy rather than your conscious mind.

The next exercises to allow your pendulum to swing without any conscious influence

You need 3 coins.
Put 2 coins on a table with a little space inbetween them.
Hold your pendulum above them between the two coins.
Wait a few moments. Allow the pendulum to start making its own pattern between them. It might for instance swing in a figure of eight.

Once you establish its pattern, take one of the coins away and replace it with the third coin.

Repeat above.
What does the pendulum do?
Now put the original coin back.
What does the pendulum do?

When the original coin is returned the pendulum should change the pattern of its swing and return to the original pattern.

Numbers Exercise

Ask a friend to think of a number between 1 and 20.
Ask the pendulum what number your friend is thinking.
Repeat this exercise a few times to see how many you get right.

Cards Exercise

Take a traditional deck of cards.
Now ask your pendulum to separate the red and black cards.
Hold your pendulum over the pile of cards and ask about the top card. Ask 'Is the top card red?' … Do you get yes or no?
Place the cards the pendulum gets correct in a pile as you work through the deck.
At the end of the exercise count how many cards the pendulum got correct.
Repeat this exercise a few times and the pile of cards the pendulum got correct should get larger.

Objects Exercise

Pick three or four objects and put them on a table.

Turn your back and ask a friend to pick up and hold one of the objects for about 15-20 seconds, then replace it.

Turn around again then hold your pendulum above each object and ask 'is this the object your friend held?'

When your pendulum gives a 'yes' response, ask your friend if you got it correct.

Psychic Workout (revision)

Important before you start on any kind of psychic work is grounding and protection.

These are the basic practices you need to get into the habit of carrying out regularly.

There are many different methods to ground and protect and some have already been described. If you are new to this, experiment until you find the ones that you feel comfortable with.

Protection

Remember that in psychic work we need to take responsibility for protecting our energy field. Our energy field is our first line of defence. So the purpose of protection is to block out negative vibrations/energy that comes from outside sources. For this:

Close your eyes and calm your thoughts

Imagine a white bubble of light surrounding you from head to toe

The bubble should extend above your head and below your feet

Set the intention that this bubble of energy is strong all around you

Know that anything from the outside that touches your bubble will move around it like the wind moving around a solid object

Know that this shield is around you constantly and moves with you without hindrance

If you find it difficult to visualise the above, setting the intention is all that is required in energy work. Set the intention and trust you will be protected.

Three
How to Use your Pendulum
Asking Questions of your Pendulum

Before using your Pendulum to give readings you know now that it has to be cleansed. You might hold your pendulum under running water for a few moments to dispel and remove negative energy.

You can test it again for yes/no answers until you feel more bonded with your pendulum or you might feel confident from your previous exercises that you understand the language of your pendulum.

If you want to re-set your pendulum to determine its yes/no response, ask a question you know a 'yes' answer to and notice its rotation then ask a question that will have a 'no' answer and notice how your pendulum responds. You may notice that for a yes it circles in a clockwise direction and for a no it circles anti-clockwise, or it may swing backwards and forwards. Eventually you will be tuned into its response to your questions.

And now the fun begins.

Once you feel confident that you can 'read' your pendulum you are ready to ask it questions you do not know the answer to.

When asking a question you want an answer to, remain still. Some people believe that the pendulum becomes an extension of the person or the subconscious of the person who uses it and the movement of the pendulum comes from your Higher Self. Be still. Be quiet and be patient.

Keep your question as specific as possible.

Only ask questions that require a Yes/No answer.

Try to keep your mind clear and remain calm so your answers will be accurate and unbiased.

So, when using your Pendulum to receive answers you need to phrase your questions so there can be a yes/no or maybe response. It is important to structure your question carefully. – I know I am repeating myself but often in our workshops, we see people phrasing their questions wrongly and this can only lead to frustration, both for you when trying to read your pendulum and for the person you are reading for.

Specific questions will get the best answers. Questions such as Will I ever find happiness? or Will I ever find my Soul Mate? is nowhere near specific enough. Should I stay or should I go?, is another example of a poor question. The question should be: Should I stay? Or it should be: Should I go? One or the other. Aim to phrase it so you get a specific yes/no answer.

You can ask your pendulum about choices, for instance: According to current energies around me, should I attend the Reiki Workshop? Or: According to current energies around me, should I buy a new computer?

Asking your pendulum to predict who you will marry could lead to disappointment. The future isn't set in stone. Instead, you might ask: Is my relationship with Ken for my highest good at this particular time?

Some people use their pendulums to predict future children or the sex of a baby. This is an area where there are differences in opinion as this would be a prediction. Predicting the future accurately is difficult because it is based on probability. Also in questions like these, consider moral, ethical and legal issues especially if you intend to use your pendulum for giving professional readings.

When asking about the future: we all make our own choices. We have free will. The pendulum might say you will marry George but you can choose not to marry George in which case your future would be very different than had the marriage taken place!

When you use your pendulum to make predictions, the answer could well be based on your own subconscious hopes and wishes or your expectations, thus giving answers you might want to hear.

You can ask your pendulum about your health i.e. Is overwork causing my headaches? Do I need to relax more?

You can work through your chakras asking: Is my root chakra balanced? Is my Sacral Chakra balanced? etc.

Other ways to use your pendulum for health includes holding it over crystals to help you choose which one might be appropriate to help heal energy blockages in the aura or chakras.

You could ask your questions about gifts you are choosing for friends i.e. Would Joe like these socks for his birthday?

If you are planning a barbecue you might ask about weather conditions. You could for instance ask: will the Sun be shining on Thursday? Or more specifically, include the time on Thursday when you will be lighting up your barbecue!

Now that you are asking your pendulum questions you do not know the answer to, you could use this as an exercise to test your pendulum, writing down the answers in your psychic journal and checking later on how accurate the pendulum's answer has been.

Examples of how you might phrase questions for your pendulum:

>Is ….. for my highest good as a friend?

Is …. for my highest good as a partner?

Should I buy the red car?

Is ….. the right place for me to travel to?

The pendulum will connect to what is for your highest good at this moment in your life. But remember also that you have your own free will. You make your own choices and you should not let the pendulum make your choices for you. Instead use it for guidance and to help you consider what your next move should be.

Have fun and practice, practice, practice!

EXAMPLE QUESTONS TO ASK YOUR PENDULUM

– Notice how these are worded to receive a yes/no response.

RELATIONSHIPS:

Can I trust (person's name)?

Is (person's name) being honest with me?

Would it be good for me to date (person's name)?

Shall I call (person's name)?

Is (person's name) in a relationship?

Is (person's name) and I spiritually compatible?

Is (person's name) and I emotionally compatible?

At this present time, will (person's name) be a good match for me?

WORK:

Is (fill in blank) the best course of action?

Can I trust (colleague's name)?

Will this (name it) venture be successful?

Should I apply for an interview?

Is it time to look for a new job?

Is (name) a good company to work for?

Will this be a good opportunity?

MONEY:

Will I find a buyer for (item you are selling)?

Is this purchase (name it) a good choice for me?

Is this a good time to sell (name item)?

Is this a good deal?

Should I wait for an item (name the item) to be discounted?

Do I really need to buy this (name the item)?

HEALTH:

Am I doing too much for other people?

Am I being too lazy?

Is this food (name the food) good for me to eat?

Do I have any allergies?

Should I get another opinion?

Should I make an appointment with the doctor?

Is this a good diet (name the diet you are referring to) for me?

Do I need to exercise more?

Am I allergic to (name food)?

Is this condition hereditary?

FINDING LOST ITEMS:

Is (item) in the house?

Is (item) in the car?

Did I leave (item) at work?

Is (item) in the bedroom? ... Go through other rooms.

Is (item) nearby?

Is (item) clearly visible?

Are my glasses in the drawer?

Has someone taken (item)?

What if my Pendulum Doesn't Work?

This is a question often asked by people who are new to using pendulums and there will be times when your pendulum might seem to give confusing responses or wrong answers to your questions. These are some of the reasons why this might happen:

- Are you tense, tired or mentally exhausted?
- Are you finding it hard to trust you can do this?
- Are you feeling negative?

- Are you allowing your conscious expectations to intrude? – This can be the hardest challenge to conquer in any kind of psychic work. Try to blank your mind so you are linking only with your Higher Self.

- Check you aren't too close to electrical appliances. The high frequency could affect your pendulum.

- Have you phrased your question to give a specific yes/no answer?

- Are you being too impatient? Sometimes you have to wait a while to receive the answer.

If you still feel you are getting wrong answers, try cleansing your pendulum, activate the pendulum again with your energy and re-program your pendulum. The main thing to remember is: like every skill and ability, it takes regular practice. We can't expect to get instant great results. Relax, keep an open mind and be willing to put time and effort into this. The more you practice, the better your pendulum skills will be.

Four
The Many Uses of a Pendulum

How Pendulums can be used to find missing items, answer questions and to detect weaknesses in the body

We have already discussed some of the many uses for your pendulum. In this chapter I will go into this in more detail.

Dowsing is a form of clairvoyance that has been used for centuries to find water, answer questions or predict the sex of a child, depending on the dowsing tool. – It has to be mentioned that if you ever choose to use your pendulum for professional readings, for legal reasons it is not recommended that you predict births, future children, answers to legal questions or specific health questions.

Pendulums can be used to help balance Chakras or for homing in on health problems but if used for health, it should be alongside traditional medical advice/treatment.

Medical dowsers use a pendulum which has been tested and proven to work and the theory is: your Higher Self knows what is good for your health and how each internal organ works and a medical dowser can clairvoyantly pick up these same factors about others.

The Pendulum or Dowsing Tool (Revision)

Anyone can make a simple dowsing tool; there is no need to spend a fortune on anything fancy.

As already mentioned, all that is necessary is a pendulum or something to act as one, such as a ring, on the end of a chain or piece of thread. The chain should be held between thumb and first finger so the pendulum is freely suspended in the air and then the dowsing tool can be tested.

Test your dowsing tool every day by asking questions with known answers such as "Am I a woman?" Note the way the pendulum moves. Most people find it moves clockwise for "yes" but this isn't always the case. Your pendulum will respond to your energy vibration. Then ask a question to which the answer is "no"; this is often signified by an anti-clockwise movement, however, again, not always, and as already recommended, each person should check to find their own polarities.

A movement should also be discerned for "don't know" answers, which could, for instance be moving backwards and forwards.

Dowsing for Health

One way to dowse for health might be to go through a list of vitamins and minerals and ask "Have I sufficient Vitamin A in my body?" Note the result in your psychic journal and continue through other vitamins and minerals such as calcium zinc, iron, sodium, potassium etc.

Another question could be: "Have I too much Sodium (or any other vitamin or mineral) in my body?" If the answer is yes, it could be that you have a high amount of sodium due to an excessive intake of salt. Or consider the reasons why you may have a high level of other vitamins/minerals and whether this is healthy for you.

After going through the vitamins and minerals, new questions can be added and from the answers, health can be improved through for instance, eating more fresh fruit if there is a lack of Vitamin C in the body.

Dowsing and Homeopathic Medicine

Many homeopathic practitioners are now using Dowsing as a way to compliment what they already use and know. Homeopathic remedies are in the main from plants with healing energies derived from the cosmos. Dowsing can help the practitioner identify possible problems and when remedies are administered, this will enhance the natural healing and balance of an individual's energy.

Map Dowsing

Map dowsing can and has been used to find water sources, mineral ores, to locate people, lost pets or objects. Map dowsers use a pendulum and a map or they might use dowsing rods. Use of a map will mean the dowser is able to locate a specific area without having to travel to the site. – A monk in France, Abby Mermet, for instance, used map dowsing to find oil and gas wells in South America and the results were 90% positive even though, so it is told, he did not set foot outside France!

Tools needed for map dowsing are: a map or drawing of the area, and your pendulum, a ruler and a pencil.

Firstly state what you are looking for. Now slowly slide the ruler across the map or drawing while at the same time asking the pendulum to indicate when the straight edge of your ruler is at the target.

When your pendulum indicates that the ruler is at the target, with your pencil, draw a straight line across the map.

Now turn your ruler 90 degrees so you are going to move up/down the line you have drawn. Begin to slide the ruler across the map or drawing while at the same time asking your pendulum to indicate when the ruler is at the target.

Draw a straight line across the map and where the lines meet, this will be the location you are looking for.

Dowsing For Treasure

Is it possible to dowse for treasure? Well, some people spend a fortune on metal detectors and spend days, weeks and months walking fields, beaches and other areas searching for 'treasure'.

Using a pendulum or divining rods, there is no reason why people can't at least try to dowse for treasure. Jim Longton from Lancashire, England, took up dowsing after retiring and in 1990 found a hoard of Viking silver brooches valued at over £42,000. Jim also managed to pinpoint a 350 year-old sunken ship "The Blessing of Burntisland" through map dowsing. He identified the co-ordinates on a map with a pendulum and later chose exactly the same spot while using dowsing rods.

Dowsing for Lost Pets

Map dowsing can also be used to locate lost pets or people. For this type of dowsing it is best to dowse as soon as possible after the animal or person's disappearance. Use the animal or person's name while dowsing and hold an image of them in your mind so as not to pick up on other similar energies in that area. Some map dowsers will hold an item belonging to the pet/person while dowsing to help strengthen the connection.

Dowsing for Water

Water divining is an ancient art to locate water in fields and other areas, using divining tools such as a bent rod or forked twig. … It is actually possible to making diving rods out of an old metal coat hanger. In Cumbria in the UK some older farmers will still use this amazing skill to find water sources. The dowser will walk, holding his rod or twig in front of him and the stick will rotate or start pointing downwards. Your pendulum can also be used to find water.

What else can you use your pendulum for?

Pendulum dowsing can be used for many different things and including those already discussed, pendulums can be used for:

Finding lost objects
Finding Water
Finding Treasure
Finding lost pets and lost people
Finding gas mains or leaks
Sexing un-hatched eggs
Dowsing fruit and vegetables to find out how fresh they are
Testing food supplements for compatibility with your body
Balancing Chakras
Answering questions on love, relationships, career, money
House hunting
Dating i.e. if single, asking 'is this the person I should go out with?'
Choosing educational courses
As a lie-detector

Psychic Workout

Exercise to find Water and other Objects

Go out into your garden or into the street where you think there might be a water pipe. Ask your pendulum to respond with a yes when you are over a water pipe. Or if you are in your garden, just ask your pendulum to respond with a yes when you walk over a water course. It can be fun noticing the different responses of your pendulum. – You can ask your pendulum to locate anything. Ask a friend to hide something in the garden then see if you can find it with your pendulum.

Exercise – Finding a hidden object

Ask a friend to hide an object somewhere in your house. Once done, set the intention with your pendulum that you would like to use it to find the object.

As you go through each room, ask your pendulum if the item is hidden in that room. If the answer is no, move on to the next room.

If it is a Yes, stay in the room. In each of the four corners of the room, ask if the object is close.

Once you get a Yes response, ask the pendulum if the object is at floor level. If no, you will know to look a little higher.

Search inside cupboards, drawers, around that corner. Ask more questions of your pendulum if need be, until you find the object.

Get to know your Pendulum

Get to know your Pendulum by carrying it with you when you are travelling or if you're going on holiday.

Travel and a change of scenery often gives us a chance to 'switch off', relax and to be alone in a quiet, peaceful place. Whether it is in a hotel room, on a beach, in a park or try to find a few minutes each day to be alone with your pendulum. This can help heighten your psychic sensitivity and strengthen your link with your divining tool.

Pendulum and Pets

If you have a pet, whether it is a cat, dog, horse or hamster, hold your Pendulum over the head (or body in the case of a small animal) of your pet. Ask your pendulum: Is my pet feeling happy today? … and observe your Pendulum's swing.

Pendulum and Plants

At different times of the day hold your Pendulum over a house plant and observe its swing. You might also try holding your Pendulum over a house plant before feeding it. Observe what it does. Now give the plant some water. Hold your Pendulum over the plant a few minutes after it has been given the water and observe what occurs.

Pendulum and Food

Hold your Pendulum over a healthy food such as fresh fruit or vegetable and ask "Is this food beneficial to my health?" Observe its swing. Hold your Pendulum over non-healthy food and ask the same question. Notice the difference in the Pendulum's swing.

These exercises will help you bond with your Pendulum.

Points to Ponder

List three different uses for your Pendulum and how you would approach giving a reading for each subject.

Revision – Testing your Pendulum

Remember to test your pendulum regularly or when using new pendulums by asking it questions to which you know the answer.

Be sure you are relaxed.
Clear your thoughts.
Hold your pendulum in front of you as you have already learned to do and then ask questions such as:

Is today a Tuesday?
Is my name George?
Am I female?
Do I like chocolate?
Is my favourite colour green?
Is it autumn?

… Ask a range of questions for which there will be a definite yes/no answer.
Be concise and clear about the questions.

Your pendulum should swing in the directions that confirm your yes/no answers. If your pendulum does not seem to answer correctly, cleanse and recharge your pendulum.

Five
How do you Approach Pendulum Dowsing?
Tips for Using your Pendulum

Your approach to pendulum dowsing can have a big effect on how successful you become as a pendulum dowser. It is, for instance, important to approach this subject with an open mind. You might be sceptical about how dowsing works but it does work and the more you try it, the more likely it is that you will discover this for yourself. But you must be open about it. – Everything in this universe is 'energy' including you. And just as a radio picks up information from invisible radio waves, your pendulum can be looked on as being a powerful antenna that receives information from the energy vibrations in the environment.

A good way to approach pendulum dowsing is to look on it as a new and exciting learning experience. It is a great way to increase your awareness, intuition, psychic ability, knowledge and understanding. Anyone can learn pendulum dowsing but it does take constant practice. There will be times when your pendulum does not seem responsive. Perhaps this is a sign it needs to be cleansed or the energy isn't right for you on this particular day. Cleanse your pendulum and try again tomorrow …. Be willing to keep trying.

Here I may repeat lessons of the past few chapters. This serves as a revision and helps important aspects of spiritual practice to be filed in your mind. I have found in our workshops that even though it has been explained, often a number of times, questions will be asked that had already been previously answered. I find it can be helpful therefore, to repeat important aspects of a subject to help learners understand and remember it well.

Tips for using your Pendulum

Length of Chain: the more you practice dowsing the more you will realise that there is a place to hold your chain where you will get a quicker response. To find this, slowly work your finger and thumb up and down the chain until you feel the strongest response. This is usually about two to six inches up from the pendulum.

Is the size of the swing important? Some dowsers will have a small swing when using their pendulum, others will have an active pendulum which goes in wide circles. The motion does not matter. What matters is that your pendulum works for you.

Which type of chain? Chains, thread, fine cord, fishing line, fine wool, dental floss can all be used to make a pendulum.

Which type of Pendulum? There are many different types of pendulum so do take time choosing the one that feels right for you. If you're out and about and you don't have your pendulum at hand but would like to find the answer to a question, you can use any small item, such as a bead (not too light), paperclip, ring or crystal tied onto the end of a piece of string. – Make sure the item isn't too light. You need some weight in order to distinguish the different movements of the swing. When choosing a pendulum, remember to pay attention to the one that you feel particularly drawn to … the pendulum that 'speaks' to you.

When pendulum dowsing always use your Dominant Hand: When using some dowsing tools it is recommended that you use your non-dominant hand but for pendulums, use your dominant hand and gently pinch the chain between your thumb and pointer finger. Your grip should be relaxed so the pendulum can hang without any tension.

Cleanse, Ground and Shield before using your Pendulum and Afterwards:

As in all psychic work, before using your pendulum for yourself or to answer questions for someone else, spend a few minutes cleansing, grounding and shielding.

For psychic cleansing, you might visualise yourself standing under a waterfall and know that the water is washing any negativity in your body away. To ground yourself, you might imagine roots coming out of your feet, going down deep into the earth below. See your roots wrap securely around a large boulder or crystal deep inside the earth. Know that you are grounded. To shield and protect yourself from negative energies in your environment or that may be invading your aura, visualise yourself being surrounded by a bubble of white or blue light. These are important routines to get into in all psychic work and should be carried out daily.

Wording of Questions: Remember to think carefully about how to word your questions. They need to be clear and not vague.

Focus on the Question: When using your pendulum you need to focus your mind on the question you want answered. Don't let other thoughts get in the way. … Practising meditation can help you learn how to control your thoughts.

Ask your Pendulum for permission to practice. Do not misuse your pendulum. Your intention should be to use it only for the highest good of yourself and/or others.

Are you influencing the Answers? If you feel you might in some way, subconsciously, be influencing the answers, ask a friend for questions they know the answers to and see if you still get the right answers.

If reading for other people respect their privacy. Try to help them without interfering. Remember too that you can give guidance on what the pendulum advises but you should never make choices or decisions on another person's behalf. They need to be given the space to make their own mind up.

Ill health, tiredness, stress, noise and disturbances around you can all make a difference to your answers. If you aren't relaxed the answers are likely to be unreliable.

Be humble. Never boast about the success of your psychic work. Give thanks to the Universe, the angels, your Spirit Guides ... whomever or whatever you believe to be helping you.

What might affect the response from the Pendulum?

If you don't feel your pendulum is giving an accurate response, there are a number of reasons for this including:

Poor Communication: Is your question clear or is it vague? Think about how you are phrasing your question. Don't, for instance, just ask "Is this vitamin good for me?" Be more precise. If it is going to be good, in what way? Vitamins can have both good and bad aspects, for example, a vitamin might address general diet deficiencies but in some instances taking vitamin supplements can trigger a health condition or make an existing health condition worse. So state the question clearly, for example "Will this vitamin serve my highest good?" or "Will this vitamin help keep my digestive system healthy?"

Tiredness can make it difficult for you to focus or knock your intuition out of balance

Wrong Timing: You might be using your pendulum even though the time or conditions may not be right for this particular question

Forcing an Answer: You might desire a certain answer so strongly that you are subconsciously influencing the swing of the pendulum

Being Off-Balance: If you are feeling emotionally, physically or mentally out of kilter it is not advisable to try reading with your Pendulum

Wrong focus: Instead of focusing on the question, you are focusing too hard on the pendulum itself

Electrical Interference: If you are too close to electrical equipment, their frequency might interfere with the reading

Points to Ponder

Think about how to word questions when giving a Pendulum reading and give some example questions you might ask your Pendulum.

Six
Giving Pendulum Readings
What to Consider when Giving Pendulum Readings to Others

Unless you are practising within a group of like-minded others, it is not a good idea to offer to give people pendulum readings for the fun of it. Wait until you have had plenty practice before trying to read for other people. Start by bonding with your pendulum and reading for yourself, try the exercises in this book and once you feel you have enough experience, offer to give readings to close friends.

When reading for other people you need to make a psychic link with that person. The pendulum picks up energy from the person you are reading for and therefore you need to make a good connection in order to gain a reliable answer. Many people find it easier to use the pendulum for themselves than for others. So don't get too disheartened if your first attempts to give a pendulum reading for others aren't very successful. Eventually you will learn to get a stronger connection and to pick up their energy more accurately.

When reading for others, don't forget to ground, cleanse and shield before and after giving a reading. Approach the reading in the same way you would be reading for yourself by asking the questions for 'name the person' and focusing on the question.

Preparing to Give a Pendulum Reading for Others and Giving a Pendulum Reading

So, now that you have a good understanding of how your Pendulum works, you know how to approach giving a Pendulum reading for yourself and you have a good bond with your Pendulum, you might feel ready to give readings to others.

Before reading for others, it can help to develop your own private ritual in order to set the mood for the reading and help you relax and connect with your Spirit Guides, Angels or Higher Self as feels right for you.

You might have a special place in your home where you like to conduct your readings. Prepare the environment so this too, helps you get into the right mood to use your Pendulum. ... Burn incense, light candles, turn the lights low, play relaxing music.

Spend some minutes meditating. State the intention of forming a link with your Pendulum in order to give readings for the highest good of yourself and others. Now swing the Pendulum and focus on its swing for about 30 seconds, allow yourself to ignore distractions, allow the tension in your body to be released and feel yourself relax.

Pendulum Exercise – Performing a Phone Pendulum Reading for a Friend

One way to practice reading for other people is to ask a friend if you can give them a Pendulum reading over the phone.

This will give you practice in linking with a person who isn't in the room with you. Conduct the reading as you would if your friend was sitting in front of you. Remember to reword the questions others ask of you if necessary in order to make them more clear. You need to be in a state of relaxation and concentration as you begin your Pendulum reading.

Seven
Pendulum Charts and Alphabet

How to Design Pendulum Charts and How to Use the Alphabet with your Pendulum

Sometimes when you are dowsing you might want to make a choice between a number of options. For instance: which crystal to use for meditation, which vitamins might be good for you or where would be a good holiday destination?

We can ask individual questions that are designed to give a yes/no/maybe answer or we might choose to use a chart that allows the pendulum to indicate an answer from a variety of possibilities.

Charts can be designed for specific purposes. They allow you to use your pendulum to select between a wider range of options and this can also be a quicker process than the limiting yes or no or maybe answers.

You can experiment when designing your own charts and they can be as detailed or elaborate as you want them to be.

Charts should be divided equally into the number of sections needed.

How to Make a Pendulum Chart

Firstly decide on the theme of your chart, for example: Relationships, Health, Chakras, Career or Crystals

Think of questions you might ask on that theme.

For instance, if you're asking which crystal to meditate with, you might add to your chart: Rose Quartz, Amethyst, Amber, Jasper, Lapi Luzuli, Tourmaline, Turquoise – whichever ones you own or are drawn to.

Draw a circle or half circle on a sheet of paper.

Divide the circle/half circle into the number of sections needed relating to your questions

Draw lines at equal distances then write your options in each section.

How to use Your Pendulum Chart

Choose or design a chart that will answer the question on your mind for yourself or the person you are reading for.

Hold your pendulum above the chart where all the options meet (i.e. at the centre of the circle or semi-circle).

Relax and when you feel ready, ask the question.

The pendulum may start to swing back and forward or rotate and the swinging will become stronger.

Watch where the pendulum goes. If it seems to keep returning to a particular spot on the chart or if it won't go any further than a certain section as it is swinging, this is where the answer lies. Trust your intuition as to how this answer relates to the situation on your mind.

Ideas for Pendulum Charts:

For timing: days of the week, months of the year and/or seasons

Chakras: if asking which chakra is blocked or needs working on
To find objects ... areas of your house, of a room, etc
Which food you might be allergic to
Which food is good for you
Tarot card of the day
Crystals that you might carry on a particular day
Destinations for a holiday

The list is endless, only limited by your imagination

Using a Pendulum Chart to scan Auras and Chakras

Pendulums are sometimes used by Energy Workers and Crystal Healers to scan their clients' auras and chakras. This can help the practitioner sense disruptions to the flow of energy and gain information on active or inactive areas. Where dense energy is detected, the practitioner might recommend crystals, colours, perform reiki over the area or suggest changes in habits and behaviour to help encourage the energy to flow again.

There are a number of methods to use the pendulum in this respect. You can use a chart or you can hold the pendulum over each Chakra. You can also scan the aura using your pendulum.

To use a chart, use a purchased chart or design your own. Divide your chart into seven equal segments, each segment to relate to one of the seven main chakras. Lay the chart on a desk. Hold your pendulum at the centre. Relax. Ask your pendulum to show you which chakra is open or blocked or needs working on. You might ask for instance "Show me which chakra is blocked today," or you might ask a specific question like "Which chakra is making me feel so confused right now?"

To scan the aura with your pendulum, prepare yourself first by grounding, cleansing and shielding. Ask the person you are reading to lie in a comfortable position. Now move your pendulum slowly, up and down their body. Note how your pendulum is moving. You might notice that it moves in circles at the chakras but in a back and forth movement between chakras. Where a pendulum stops moving, this can show a problem with energy in that area. When this occurs, ask that the energy flow be corrected and when your pendulum starts moving again, continue over the rest of the body.

You might choose to use your pendulum with both a chart and body scan so you are able to compare the two readings.

You can use nutrition charts to help determine which vitamins or food supplements are needed, aromatherapy charts and charts for helping with emotional or relationship issues.

Using the Alphabet with your Pendulum

We have discussed how to use your pendulum to gain a yes/no response in a number of areas. There are ways, too, to use the alphabet to receive answers. One way to gain information from your Pendulum is to write the letters of the alphabet onto small pieces of paper or cards.

Shuffle or mix the letters around as you place them on a table in front of you with the letters facing downwards (this helps you know your mind is not influencing the pendulum's swing)

Ground and shield and hold your pendulum over the letters. Ask your question and then hover your pendulum over each letter in turn. The pendulum might start to swing, vibrate or pull downwards towards the letters that will provide the answer. Once the pendulum responds to a letter, turn it over and write it down. Then return it to the table, as the pendulum may be drawn to the same letter more than once.

When the pendulum stops reacting to the letters, take a look at your letters. What word can you form from them? Sometimes the vowels are missing and you may be able to form words by adding vowels to the consonants.

You can use the alphabet method to receive answers other than yes/no ones. To ask your Angel and Guides' names as well as the names of your household angels or healing angels who are working with you.

Eight
How to use your Pendulum for Spiritual Development

When using your pendulum for spiritual development, ground, cleanse and protect before your session with the pendulum. Set the intention that your aim is to work with your highest self to discover more about yourself. Ask your pendulum whether you have permission to connect and use the pendulum for (name the purpose) at that time.

Using your Pendulum to access the Akashic Records

The Akashic Records can be visualised as a huge library dating back to the beginning of time. This Book of Life is a memory storehouse containing the history of every soul that has ever lived since the beginning of creation. All our souls have their own Akashic record and this huge storehouse also holds collective records of our combined souls' journeys.

Before the session, you might want to prepare yourself by meditating and voicing your intention.
Ask your pendulum if you have permission to access your Akashic Records. –There are gatekeepers to the Akashic Records who must allow you entry to the information within.

You might also ask your spirit guides: "Please help me open my Akashic Records through my pendulum so I may have the wisdom to live this life with greater insight and awareness."

Once you know you have permission to access the Book of Life, you can start asking your pendulum questions in order to receive intuitive nudges as to the issue on your mind.

What kind of questions might you ask? - When consulting the Akashic records, you can ask about past lives, your soul's purpose, spirit guides, career, talents, healing. Remember to word your questions in order to receive a yes/no answer.

Example questions to ask the Akashic Records:

Do I have hidden talents?
Are there unresolved issues from past lives with relationships?
Are there unresolved emotional issues from past lives?
Do I limit myself?
Am I in the right career?
Am I using my innate skills to their full potential?
May I know about my past lives? (if the answer is yes, you might look at the suggested questions later in this chapter).
Do I know my Twin Flame?
Is my Twin Flame in this lifetime now?
Was I introduced to my Twin Flame in a past life?
Is there any healing required before I meet my Twin Flame?

Answers to your questions will be received directly from the Keepers of the Akashic Records. Once you have received your answers, you might meditate on these in order to gain deeper insight and inner guidance. As you are given your answers you might find you receive intuitive thoughts, feelings and impressions that may lead you to ask further yes/no questions of your pendulum or to meditate on specific areas. Approach the area of spiritual development with respect and good intentions and remember to thank your guides and angels for the answers given.

Past Lives

Have you lived before? – How can you use your pendulum to find out more about your past lives?

Depending on your beliefs, if this is something you are interested in, you can use your pendulum to discover more about your previous incarnations.

Ground and protect, as usual, before using your pendulum.

You will now be asking questions relating to your past lives. You will probably want to ask your own questions, for instance if you want to know whether you were seeing a past life in a dream, you will want to ask questions about it. But to get you started, here are some examples:

May I know about my past lives?
Have I lived before in another physical body?
Have I had more than one past life? (if the answer is yes, you might go on to ask questions such as: Have I lived more than two past lives? Have I lived less than ten past lives?)
Is there anything from my past lives that that would be helpful for me to know in this life?
Focusing on my first incarnation, was I male?
Focusing on my first incarnation, was I female?
Focusing on my first incarnation, was it in the first century? – go through the centuries
Was this past life in the first half (name your number) of the first century?
Was this past life in the second half of the first (name your number) century?
Did I live more than once in the first (name your number) century?

Focusing on a specific past life:
In this past life, was I a teacher? (name professions as you feel drawn)
In this past life, was I married?
In this past life, did I have brothers?

In this past life, did I have sisters?
In this past life, did I have any children?
In this past life, was I happy in my work?
In this past life, did I live in a small community?
In this past life, did I live in a city?
Are there any issues from this past life that need healing?
Am I able to heal this now?

(if the answer is yes, close your eyes and set the intention that healing be given to your past life. Hold your pendulum as you do this and wait until it stops. Ask your pendulum "is healing complete?" before moving to your next question).

Continue with your own questions, writing down the answers and in this way you can build up an impression of your past life experiences.

How your Pendulum can help your Spiritual Development

When using your pendulum to answer questions regarding your spiritual development, you might continue your session using tarot, angel or oracle cards, meditation, or other tools that will help give you further insight into any area you are focusing on.

Example questions to consider:

Regarding people who have an impact on your life:

Does (name) have a strong impact on my life? (go through friends, relatives, colleagues)
Does (name) have a positive effect on my life?
Does (name) have a negative effect on my life?

(you will want to spend more time with those who have a positive influence and avoid those who bring negativity into your life).
Have I known (name) in a past life?
Is there a soul link with (name)?

Goals:
Is it time to set new long-term goals?
Is (name the area) the right area of my life to focus on now? (you might add 'relationships', 'healing', 'mediumship', 'work', 'marriage', 'creativity' etc.)

Career:
Am I in my ideal job?
Would (name profession) be an ideal job for me?
Am I making the best use of my skills in my work?
Would I benefit through learning new skills?

Psychic Skills:
Should I develop my mediumship ability?
Am I going in the right direction?
Would I benefit from a mentor?
Should I be mentoring others?
Should I be relying more on my intuition?
Are my dreams meaningful?
Would I be a good tarot reader?
Should I study palmistry?
Should I study healing? (If yes, ask: Would Reiki be right for me? Go through a list of healing i.e. aromatherapy, crystal healing, colour healing, acupuncture, Bach Flower remedies etc.)

Note: Using your pendulum to discover information about your past lives, spiritual experiences, soul's purpose, spirit guides or inner child can trigger vivid dreams or psychic impressions. If you notice a distinct change in your dreams, emotions or thoughts after using your pendulum for spiritual development, you might consult a psychic life-coach counsellor who will give you spiritual guidance. Do not ask questions that make you feel uncomfortable. Your guides will protect you from having access to information that might cause confusion or upset in your present life.

Using your Pendulum to Balance Chakras

Working on or with your Chakras is a great way to maintain your health and well-being. You can also give Chakra readings to your friends.

If you aren't familiar with the Chakra system, these are cone-shaped energy-centres located in a line from the base of our spine to the top of our head. Chakras collect energy from Life Force Energy or Universal Energy and directs it into and around our body and our subtle bodies.

There are seven main Chakras: Root Chakra which is located at the base of our spine (Colour Red). Sacral Chakra located at the Abdomen (colour orange). Solar Plexus Chakra, located between navel and lower ribs (colour yellow). Heart Chakra, located at centre of chest (colour green). Throat Chakra, located at your throat (colour blue). Third Eye Chakra, located at centre of forehead (colour indigo). Crown Chakra located at top of your head (colour violet/white).

When using your Pendulum to detect health problems/energy blockages, it can help to keep the Pendulum close to your body for a few hours so it can soak in your energy.

Before using your pendulum, ask your Spirit Guides/Angels/Higher self to help you achieve a reading that will serve your highest good.

If you are using your pendulum to read another person's chakras, ask them to lie down on their back and relax.

Now hold the chain of your Pendulum about four to six inches (ten to fifteen cm) above their crown chakra. Observe its movement as this will help you determine whether the Chakra is open or blocked.

If the pendulum is moving clockwise, the Chakra is open and well balanced and energy is flowing freely.
If the pendulum is moving in an elliptical swing, there may be an imbalance of energy flowing into the body at that Chakra.
If the pendulum is moving erratically, it is possible your friend is not feeling relaxed and this may not be a good time to give this reading.
If the pendulum remains still, try moving its position slightly in case you are not above the Chakra. If you get the same result, there may be a blockage in that Chakra.
If the pendulum is moving anti-clockwise, the Chakra could be too open and over-active.

Observe the pendulums movements and move down through the other Chakras.

With practice and a little research on the meanings of the individual Chakras, you will be able to read your own and other people's Chakras. For this exercise, however, to keep it simple: if you find a Chakra is blocked, introduce the colour of that Chakra into your life for seven days. For instance if you have a blocked Root Chakra, wear red clothes, bring red flowers into your home, eat red food, carry a red gemstone. … more research into Chakras will give you a greater understanding of how Chakras work and how to balance your Chakras.

Find the name of your guide using a pendulum.

This is an exercise we enjoy in our workshops. It can be done solo or as part of a team.

What is the name of your Guide who is helping you currently with your psychic work?
For this exercise we are going to use a mix of intuition, help from our guides and our pendulums.
Ground and protect.
Now ask your guide to give you their name. Ask that the name be shortened if necessary so it is 8 letters or less.
Now go through the alphabet asking:
Does your name have an A in it? Yes/No
Does your name have a B in it? Yes/No
Continue through to Z

Make a note of the letters that received a Yes answer

If there are more than 8 letters, go through this list again, asking again if each letter is in the name. Once you get it down to 8 write down the letters and share them with your group.

Now everyone should join in and see if they can make a word or more than one word out of the letters. Once a number of words have been suggested, be guided by your intuition to the name you feel is your guide's.

Nine
Frequently Asked Questions about Pendulum Dowsing

You now have all the information you need to read your pendulum. In this final chapter, I am going to include questions and answers that have come up in our Pendulum workshops that you, too, might find helpful. Some of the answers come from different mentors who help in our workshops.

Q: I don't feel my pendulum and I are bonding. It keeps giving me wrong answers.

A: If after cleansing your pendulum and grounding yourself and clearing your mind you still feel you aren't getting a definite response, you might try holding the pendulum about an inch above the palm of the opposite hand that is holding the pendulum. Try first opening and closing your hands a few times and this will help activate the energy chakras in your hands. Now clear your mind and focus on your question. Keep your mind clear or your thoughts will get muddled in the energy. Once your question has been answered you can lower the pendulum to touch the palm of your other hand for a few seconds, thus signifying this question has been answered and clearing the pendulum for the next question.

Q: I have a very important question to ask my pendulum, and I don't think I'm spiritual enough. I've done everything you told me, and I'm still not sure I'm right.

Eva's answer: Are you getting consistent yes/no answers when you test your pendulum? Don't feel it's because you aren't spiritual enough. Even experienced readers can have off-days with their pendulum and it's rare to get it 100% correct. Do you read cards? It might help to ask your pendulum and ask your cards the same question if it is an important one

Q: I've been trying to really take note of my pendulum's movement. I'm noticing that mine could be working differently from others. It is showing back and forth for 'no', up and down for 'yes', circles for 'maybe'. As I'm noticing this direction change happening, I am wondering whether I'm reading it wrongly. May I ask: does everyone's pendulum answer back and forth, up and down or not? Is there rotation to the swinging, if that makes sense?

Corinne's Answer: Pendulums respond differently for each individual according to their energies and vibrations. This is why it's important to bond with your pendulum so you can understand the language it uses to speak to you. Ask for your yes/no/maybe answers until you feel certain of these. Make your questions clear and simple and the more you hold your pendulum and work with it, the stronger it will come.

Q: Is it bad luck to use a pendulum on a Sunday? I feel I shouldn't use mine on Sundays.

Corinne's Answer: Each to their own. You can choose to use your pendulum whenever you feel comfortable. Many people do use theirs on a Sunday and don't feel it brings them bad luck. Do what feels right for you.

Q: I've made my own pendulum since I don't have one and it's not seeming to work for me. I tried making a few other homemade ones to see if it's the pendulum that's problem. I tried the deck of cards experiment to tell if it's yes or no, red or black. I keep getting it wrong and it seems to be such a clear answer it's giving me. I tried over my palm but it doesn't seem to respond ... well I don't feel it did. I don't know what I'm doing wrong. I can ask it questions that I know are 'yes' and 'no' and get clear answers, but for the questions other people ask, I am not doing well.

Julie's answer: Please, don't think because you have a homemade pendulum that this is causing the problem. Personally you cannot get better than a pendulum that has been made especially for you .... And even better by your own hand and with your own beautiful and unique energy. My answers to your question are:

1. If you say the answers are clear but are not right ... It just may be that you have got the answers the wrong way round i.e. circling to the left may currently be YES for you but in fact for your pendulum it's NO (this is often the case if you say your answers are clear and the opposite when doing test runs).

2. And this is sooo important .... Relax! Take it easy , bond with your pendulum ... I find ALL tools have a relationship with us (you only have to ask my husband ... I talk to my crystal ball and care and respect my regular cards like they were worth thousands). It's not a contest and some people do take a while to bond with and trust the pendulum (or any tool).

They used to say your first ever pendulum should be gifted to you but to actually make your own ... Well that has got to bring in a bond straight away. So don't give up !

And 4. Lastly ... Remember this may not be for you ... We can all have a go at tools (that is all they are) ... Some of us will excel with cards, some with psychometry, some with tea leaves ... we all are unique. Just have a go ... It may just be it's not your thing but it is enjoyable to try it and excellent in spiritual development.

Q: I don't feel I'm getting good answers from my pendulum. Am I doing something wrong?

Eva's Answer: Try to relax. Many of us don't get correct answers 100%. I would suggest (if you haven't already) that you sit with your pendulum in your hands and quieten your mind (getting into a meditative state), then ask the question: Is your pendulum is willing to work with you? If you get a 'no', put it aside for a while. If it is 'yes', you can continue with your session. You might have instant yes/no thoughts on this too.

Remember, it's very important to cleanse your mind and pendulum every time you start working with it. – Some practitioners take time between asking questions and they cleanse their pendulum each time (between questions) because energy can get attached to it so easily.

Ask whether your mind is influencing the answer. If you feel your mind is pushing the pendulum to move the way you want it to, step back, cleanse, ground and protect, then try again.

Do you feel your pendulum is the right tool to work with at this current time? Are you having a bad day and might it not be the right time to work with your pendulum?

Q: At my mediumship class last week, I mentioned I'm learning how to work with pendulums. My mentor told me to stay away from them as I am going to be a fabulous medium and to lay off my pendulum and cards. But I enjoy working with cards and pendulum. It's going to take a long time for me to learn mediumship and I need a little help from you guys about what I should do.

A: Personally, if I enjoy using certain tools and find they help me with my psychic work, I would pursue them 'til I felt ready to stop or move on to something else. I'd question too anyone's prediction (whether a guide or person) that you're going to be a 'fabulous medium' ... this is putting a lot of pressure on you to live up to this kind of expectation of you and we can all only do our best to be the best we can according to our own abilities. I can't see any harm in experimenting with pendulum, cards or other tools. Within our groups and courses we do this all the time as it all helps your psychic development and in turn, helps your mediumship ability too. Be sure to ground, cleanse and shield regularly.

Julie's Answer: My first ever development group was run by a formal Tutor from Arthur Finlay College. Their tutors are mediums who teach development by allowing us to use all the different tools i.e cards, crystal balls, pendulums, trance tents etc. It is all to enrich us and for us to gain experience and knowledge from. It gives us a foundation and is enjoyable... especially as people develop together. Most importantly I personally feel like Carole ... you have to go with how YOU feel and what YOU want. Follow your own intuition and instincts. If you want to use a tool then use a tool and enjoy!

Q: I enjoyed the pendulum games. Out of the questions I had eight wrong and four right. Most of the ones I answered was over a notebook, then I used my pendulum over my palm. It seemed to move more. The only thing I want to know (if anyone has the answer to) is: what does it mean when the pendulum kind of sits still but vibrates at the point? I was using it myself practising with it and it vibrated instead of answering a few times?

Amber's Answer: Try to reword and if that still happens, then maybe the pendulum is telling you it is not time to know or the answer is not available at this point in time.

Q: I am making my own pendulum. Is the weighted object to use to come to a point at the end of it? Would a key be okay or a ring, but this is round?

A: It can be rounded or have a point to it. A pointed pendulum will be better when using pendulum charts while a rounded one can be good for yes/no answers.

Thank you for reading. I hope you have had as much fun learning about and experimenting with your pendulum as we do in our workshops.

If you enjoyed this book, further books by this author can be found at:
Amazon.co.uk – Carole Somerville
Amazon.com – Carole Somerville

Printed in Great Britain
by Amazon